CONTENTS

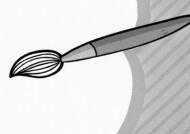

Argh m'hearties!

Come join us on a crafty adventure where you can create all the pirate-y things you need to be the captain of the Seven Seas.

Pirates are well known for sailing the world's oceans and committing crimes along the way; stealing from ships and looking for buried treasures on tropical islands dotted around the Seven Seas. The most famous pirates were from the Caribbean in the 17th and 18th centuries, but there were even pirates in Viking times – and some still exist today!

HAPPY EVER CRAFTER

PIRATES

ANNALEES LIM

Published in paperback in Great Britain in 2020 by
Wayland
Copyright © Hodder and Stoughton 2018

Senior Commissioning Editor: Melanie Palmer
Design: Square and Circus
Illustrations: Supriya Sahai

Additional illustrations: Freepik

ISBN 978 1 5263 0714 9

MIX
Paper from
responsible sources
FSC® C104740
FSC
www.fsc.org

Printed in Dubai

Wayland
An imprint of
Hachette Children's Group
Part of Hodder and Stoughton
Carmelite House
50 Victoria Embankment
London EC4Y 0DZ

An Hachette UK Company
www.hachette.co.uk

SAFETY INFORMATION:
Please ask an adult for help with any activities
that could be tricky, involve cooking or handling
glass. Ask adult permission when appropriate.

Due care has been taken to ensure the activities
are safe and the publishers regret they cannot
accept liability for any loss or injuries sustained.

You won't need to spend all of your pieces of eight on expensive craft supplies – these crafts are made from things you can find around the house, using recycled materials or things you will have in your craft box. Follow the step-by-step instructions and you can impress your shipmates with your handmade costumes, decorations, gifts and more!

FACT!

There is no evidence to suggest that pirates kept parrots as pets. It was first mentioned in the story **Treasure Island** in which Long John Silver kept a pet parrot, Captain Flint, on his shoulder. Ever since then this has been linked to all pirates.

TOP TIP

Recycling and reusing unwanted things is a great way to make your craft project environmentally friendly. Always wash old food containers or fabric before you start using them. You can also collect old envelopes, birthday cards and cardboard boxes instead of buying reams of new paper. Don't forget to ask an adult before you take anything you see lying around the house - it might not be ready for the recycling bin just yet!

DARING DRESSING UP!

Whether you need a costume for Halloween or for your very own fancy dress party, you will find the perfect pirate project here. All of these costumes can be made without threading a single needle and can be made mostly from the recycled materials you have collected.

PIRATE HAT

Pirates were out in the open seas for weeks and months at a time, so a hat was an important way to keep them cool from the sun. Make your own simple hat that will look great with the Pirate Crew outfit on page 9.

YOU WILL NEED:
- THIN CARD • MAGAZINES
- PAINT • PAINTBRUSH • SCISSORS
- STICKY TAPE • RULER

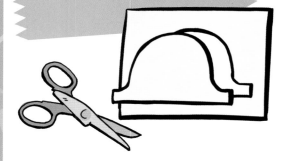

1. Cut out three identical hat shapes from the thin card that are at least 35-40 cm long and 20 cm high.

2. Use more thin card to make a headband that is big enough to fit around your head.

3. Staple the three shapes to the headband, then each shape together at the ends.

4. Paint the hat black and leave to dry.

5. Decorate with a skull and crossbones made from the white paper. Attach some feathers made from colourful magazine pages.

SAILING SHIP

The typical ships of the 14th to 17th centuries were built to carry about 40 people, but if they were stolen to be pirate ships the pirates would squeeze up to double the amount of people on board. Don't worry though, this costume is built just for one, so you will have plenty of room!

YOU WILL NEED:
- LARGE CARDBOARD BOX • PAINT
- PAINTBRUSH • FABRIC • SCISSORS
- PLAIN T-SHIRT • NEWSPAPER
- STICKY TAPE

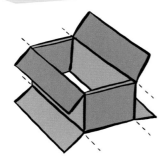

1. Cut off the top and bottom flaps of your box. Save these bits for other craft projects.

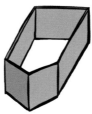

2. Make a crease at the front of the box so that it forms a point.

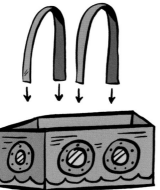

3. Paint the cardboard box to look like the ship's hull. Attach two long pieces of fabric to the cardboard with tape to make a pair of braces. These should be long enough so that you can put them over your shoulders.

4. Paint some sails and flags on to a plain T-shirt. Make sure you place some newspaper inside the T-shirt before you start to paint.

PIRATE HOOK

The most famous fictional pirate who had a hook for a hand is Captain James Hook from the book *Peter Pan* by J M Barrie. In the story Peter cuts off Hook's hand and feeds it to a ferocious crocodile.

YOU WILL NEED:

- PLASTIC BOTTLE (ABOUT 2 LITRES) • SCISSORS • STICKY TAPE • TIN FOIL • WHITE CRAFT GLUE • BLACK PAPER (OR MAGAZINE PAGES) • THIN CARDBOARD
- RULER • PENCIL

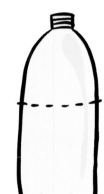

1. Cut the top 10 cm off the bottle and cover the edges with sticky tape to cover any sharp bits.

2. Cut the thin card so that it is 3 cm wide and longer that the width of the bottle.

3. Stick the card strip across the inside of the bottle to make a handle.

4. Mould the foil into the shape of the hook and stuff it into the neck of the bottle. Tape in place.

5. Use glue to cover the base and stick on some torn up pieces of black paper. Leave to dry.

PIRATE CREW

There were many people on board pirates ships, all with different jobs. As well as sailors, there were cooks, surgeons and even carpenters. Join the pirate gang by dressing up and you'll fit right in!

YOU WILL NEED:

- AN OLD T-SHIRT • MASKING TAPE • PAINT • PAINTBRUSH
- THIN CARD • STRING
- NEWSPAPER • HOLE PUNCH
- SCISSORS

1. Use masking tape to create a skull and crossbones design on the front of the T-shirt.

2. Put the newspaper inside the T-shirt before painting two different colours of stripes on to the front. Leave to dry before removing the masking tape and newspaper.

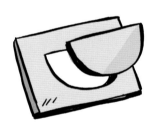

3. Draw a semi-circle shape on to some thin card for the eyepatch and cut out.

4. Punch a hole either side of the eyepatch and paint black.

DID YOU KNOW?

Many pirates wore stripes because they had often spent time in prison or in the navy, both of which had stripy uniforms!

5. Tie a piece of string to each hole. Each piece should be about 30 cm long.

PIRATE PLANS

Planning a party is so much fun, especially when you have a great theme like pirates to base it around. You might be planning a party because it is your birthday, or you may want to throw a surprise for your friends, or perhaps you just want to celebrate 'International Talk Like a Pirate' day on 19 September!

GETTING STARTED

You will find everything you need here to help you get organised and make your pirate party a success. Write down a list of things you don't want to forget or things you need to buy or make. 'X' marks the spot, so remember to check things off your list once you have done them.

PARTY TICK LIST

X **Games –** Games are lots of fun to play and you can make them extra special by giving out homemade prizes to the winners. Try using the craft ideas on page 26, and turn to page 12 for lots of game ideas.

X **Food –** Pirate adventures can work up an appetite. Look at the food ideas on page 22 for recipes to keep your crew happy.

X **Decorations –** Easily transform your party space into a cool pirate cove with the simple decoration ideas on page 17.

X **Invite People –** Send out invitations so that people remember to turn up to your party. See the invitation top tips opposite to make sure you include all the important information your guests need.

INVITATIONS

Write your invitations using this treasure map template. Make it extra special by rolling it up in an old plastic water bottle. Replace the lid with a cork to turn it into a secret message in a bottle.

Charter a course to- Say what sort of party your guests are invited to.

X marks the spot – State the address of where you are holding the party.

Ahoy there! – Write the name of the guest you are inviting.

Charter a course to

Shiver me timbers!

Set sail

Date:

Time:

AHOY THERE!

RSVP:

Shiver me timbers! – What sort of outfits do you want your guests to wear? Fancy dress, formal; you decide.

Set sail – Tell everyone when the party is happening.

RSVP – This means you would like your guests to tell you whether they can come. This helps you to plan how much food to make, how big the space needs to be and how many party bags to make.

PARTY GAMES

Lead your guests on fantastic pirate adventures with these exciting p-arrrgh-ty games. The fun doesn't just start when you begin to play, you will also enjoy making these games!

TREASURE HUNTERS

Pirates are thought to have buried their stolen treasures in remote places, such as far-off desert islands. The only way they could find them again was to mark their location on a map with an 'X'. Use this map to mark where you have hidden treasure and see whether your friends can find it!

1. Draw a map of the space you're playing in. A garden or park works best for this game.

YOU WILL NEED:

• PAPER • PENS • SCISSORS • BOX WITH LID • PLASTIC POCKET • BROWN PAPER • YELLOW PAPER • GLUE STICK

2. Place the map inside the plastic pocket (or you could use some sticky- backed plastic instead).

3. Glue brown paper on to all sides of the box using the glue stick.

HOW TO PLAY

Put sweets or a toy inside the chest. Player 1 hides this treasure (whilst Players 2 and 3 don't look) and marks it on the map with an 'X' using a dry wipe marker. Player 2 gets blindfolded and stands in the middle of the space and Player 3 uses the map to guide Player 2 to the treasure. Swap around until everyone has had a go at finding the treasure.

Why couldn't the pirate play a game of cards? Because he was sitting on the deck!

4. Attach yellow paper decorations to add the finishing touches.

5. Draw lines to make it look like a wooden treasure chest.

BURIED TREASURE

'Pieces of Eight' or 'The Eight Royals Coin' was originally a large Spanish coin made of silver which eventually became the first world currency. Make your own coins for this game and see who can be the first to uncover the treasure.

YOU WILL NEED:

- ROUND CARDBOARD CHEESE BOX
- TIN FOIL • GLUE STICK
- PERMANENT MARKER PEN
- CARDBOARD STOCK CUBE BOX
- COLOURED PAPER • PENS
- SCISSORS • SAND

1. Cover the round box in tin foil and fix in place with the glue stick.

2. Draw on to the coin using the pen. Remember, these coins usually had an '8' on them somewhere, so try hiding one in your design, too.

3. Cover the cardboard cube with coloured paper.

4. Decorate with a skull on every side. Draw either one or two bones underneath each skull.

HOW TO PLAY

Fill a large plastic storage box with sand. Ask someone who isn't playing to bury the coin in the sand. Each player takes turns to roll the dice. If it shows one bone, then the player can dig once in the sand. If it shows two bones, then they can dig twice. The first player to discover the coin is the winner.

MESSAGE IN A BOTTLE

People at sea often wrote messages, sealed them in a bottle, then cast them into the ocean. There was no way to make them reach the people they were intended for, so they were often discovered years later in different places around the world.

YOU WILL NEED:
- TEN SMALL WATER BOTTLES WITH LIDS • PAPER • PENS • SCISSORS
- PLASTIC BAG • WIRE COAT HANGER
- STRING

1. Cut up 10 pieces of paper that are just a bit shorter in size than the bottles.

2. Draw a star on one piece of paper, and a skull and crossbones on the rest.

3. Roll up each piece of paper, wrapping some string around each one. Put one scroll in each of the 10 bottles.

4. Make a hoop from a cut-up plastic bag and tie it around the neck of the bottle.

5. Bend a wire coat hanger so that it looks like a hook on a stick.

HOW TO PLAY
Fill a large plastic storage box with water and place the bottles inside. Everyone takes turns to hook a bottle and remove it from the water. The winner is the first person to find the bottle containing the scroll with the star picture.

WALK THE PLANK

As punishment, some pirates were told to walk down a plank of wood that extended out, often into shark-infested waters. Play this game to see who will survive and be crowned the captain of the ship!

YOU WILL NEED:
- MASKING TAPE • PAPER • PENS
- SCISSORS • A BLINDFOLD

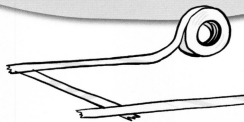

1. Use the masking tape to mark out a long plank shape in the middle of the room.

2. Draw a small island with a palm tree onto paper and cut out.

3. Draw some sharks onto paper and cut out.

FACT!
It was often thought that having females on a ship was bad luck, but this did not stop many adventurous women from becoming famous pirates.

HOW TO PLAY
Blindfold the first player and spin them round three times. Stand them at one end of the plank. The winner is the player who walks down to the other end of the plank without going into the shark infested water. If the player reaches the island, then they automatically take the lead and win.

4. Stick the sharks and island around the plank with the masking tape.

PARTY DECORATIONS

Give your party space a make over and turn it into a desert island that will be the perfect paradise for pirates.

BARRELS

Pirates and those sailing around the world would need to take lots of supplies with them on their long adventures at sea. They would often be kept in wooden barrels and rolled on to the ship because they would have been too heavy to carry.

YOU WILL NEED:

- TWO PLASTIC BOTTLES • STICKY TAPE
- BROWN PAPER • WHITE CRAFT GLUE
- GOLD CARD • SCISSORS • BLACK MARKER PEN
- GLUE STICK • PAINTBRUSH

1. Cut the two bottles in half. You just need the bottoms for this craft so you could save the tops for the Hook craft on page 8.

2. Tape the two bottle parts together with sticky tape.

3. Use the craft glue to stick some torn up brown bits of paper all around the bottle and leave to dry in a warm place.

4. Cut two gold strips and stick them around the top and bottom.

5. Write your name on the barrel.

TOP TIP
If you make 6 barrels, you could make them spell out P–I–R–A–T–E as a cool table decoration!

TREASURE CHEST

Arrange your bite-sized snacks in this treasure chest food display. Keep the lid closed to make sure your food stays fresh until you are ready to serve to your guests.

YOU WILL NEED:
- PLASTIC FOOD TRAY • PAPER • CARD
- PENS • STICKY TAPE • SCISSORS

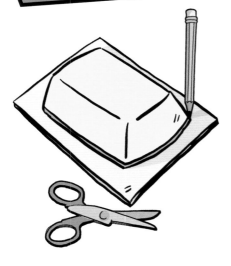

1. Draw around the edges of your plastic food tray on to a piece of paper and cut out.

2. Use this as a template to draw the base, the sides of the chest and lid on to some thin card.

3. Colour in with your pens to make them look like parts of a treasure chest - drawing planks, locks and clasps.

4. Cut out the sides and stick them together with sticky tape.

5. Make sure the food tray fits inside the base before you use the sticky tape as a hinge for the lid.

SKULL BUNTING

The Jolly Roger flag has a skull and two bones crossed over each other. It is traditionally the way to identify a pirate ship, with the flag hoisted high to scare other ships.

YOU WILL NEED:
- WHITE PAPER • PENCIL • SCISSORS
- STRING • GLUE STICK • PEN

1. Draw a skull. Then fold the piece of paper in half. Cut out and open it up.

2. Use this as a template to cut out five more identical skulls and fold them all in half.

3. Stick a loop of string in the middle of one of the folded shapes.

4. Glue the folded halves on top of each other.

5. Open up the glued stack and stick the two ends together. Draw a face on each.

TOP TIP Make lots of these and hang them together on some string to make the bunting.

PALM TREES

Upcycle broken umbrellas into beautiful palm tree decorations that you can hang from the ceiling.

YOU WILL NEED:

- AN OLD UMBRELLA • GREEN AND BROWN PAPER • SCISSORS
- STICKY TAPE

2. Cut out lots of green leaves from green paper or magazines. You could also cut up old green plastic bags.

1. Remove the fabric from the wire using some scissors. You can put these scraps aside and save them for other craft projects.

Why was the pirate ship so cheap to buy?

Because it was on sail!

3. Stick the leaf shapes on to the wires using sticky tape.

4. Cut a long strip of brown paper, or join lots of shorter strips of paper using sticky tape.

5. Tape one end of the brown paper to the top of the handle, wind it round the handle, and then fasten it to the bottom.

FACT!

Most pirates did not wear an eye patch! Some did – because they had lost an eye during a fight and they wanted to cover the injured eye with an eye patch.

TOP TIP

Tie some string to the top and use it to hook on to the ceiling. Make several palm trees and hang them close together to make a shady canopy.

PARTY FOOD

Spoil your guests with these treasured treats. Some of these recipes will need to be baked, so you will need the help of an adult. Remember to always wash your hands first!

GOLD COIN COOKIES

Gold coins were originally minted (or made) by hand, which means no two were alike. They were shaped by hand so they were never perfectly formed, unlike our coins today.

YOU WILL NEED:
- 1 CUP OF BUTTER • 1 CUP OF SUGAR • 2 CUPS OF SELF-RAISING FLOUR • WHITE CHOCOLATE CHIPS
- ICING PENS

10-15 MINUTES!

1. Place the butter and sugar in a bowl and mix together.

2. Add the flour and chocolate chips and mix by hand until it forms a dough.

4. Cook for 10-15 minutes on a medium heat, or until they are golden brown.

TOP TIP
You can always decorate pre-made cookies. This is a great activity for you and your pirate party guests to do together.

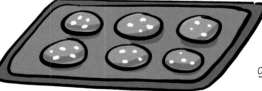

3. Roll into balls and flatten out onto a baking tray.

5. Once they have cooled, decorate them with the icing pen.

DESERT ISLAND PUNCH

YOU WILL NEED:
- CLEAN POLYSTYRENE PIZZA BASE
- BOWL • WHITE CHOCOLATE
- PUFFED WHEAT CEREAL
- GREEN FOOD DYE • CHOCOLATE
FINGER BISCUIT • GREASEPROOF
PAPER • SPOON

This delicious fruity recipe is simple to make but packs a real punch — and everyone will love the special way it is served. But best of all, it's edible, too!

1. Cut the pizza base into an oval shape.

2. Melt some white chocolate in a bowl and add a few drops of green food dye. Pour some onto a sheet of greaseproof paper to form leaf shapes, and leave to set.

Stick the chocolate finger in the middle of the mixture.

3. Melt more white chocolate in a bowl and pour in some cereal. Mix well.

4. Mould a lump of the white chocolate mixture in the middle of the base.

5. Unpeel the leaves and stick them on to the chocolate finger using more melted chocolate.

PUNCH RECIPE
Crush some blueberries and blackberries together in the bottom of a bowl. Add some lemonade and mix well. Add some cut up fruit and ice cubes. Place the floating desert island on top before serving.

GEMS AND JEWELS JELLY

This fun, multicoloured dessert tastes great and can be served in so many different ways. Place in a bowl and drizzle with cream, top with scoops of ice cream, or eat with lots of fruit.

YOU WILL NEED:
- 4 FLAVOURS OF JELLY • BOILING WATER • ICE TRAY • BOWLS • KNIFE

1. Make three different flavours of jelly and leave to set.

2. Cut them up into small pieces and mix together in a big bowl.

3. Pour the chopped jellies into ice trays.

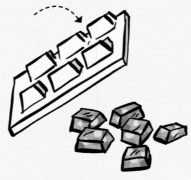

4. Make another flavour of jelly and pour into the ice trays. Leave to set.

5. Turn the tray over and tap lightly to remove the jelly from the mould. If they are stuck then dip the bottom of the tray in some warm water first.

SHIP'S WHEEL PIZZA

A ship's wheel is attached to the rudder and steers the boat. It's made from hardwood so that it does not get destroyed by the salt in the sea spray. It is usually made up of eight spokes.

YOU WILL NEED:

- PIZZA DOUGH • CHEESE
- BUTTER • GARLIC • SALT AND PEPPER • KNIFE • ROLLING PIN

2. Ask an adult to cut a star shape in the middle using the knife.

1. Roll the pizza dough out into a circle that is about 2 cm thick.

3. Place some cheese on the edge and cover it with a triangle of dough. Press down so that none of the cheese escapes when it melts.

4. Repeat with the rest of the triangles, to complete the wheel.

TOP TIP
Serve with a bowl of BBQ sauce in the middle of the wheel.

5. Melt the butter and add some chopped garlic, salt and pepper. Spread this all over the wheel evenly. Bake for 15-20 minutes or until golden brown.

CRAFTY MAKES

Transform old junk into treasures with these pirate crafts. Use them to add to the party decorations found on page 17, as prizes for the games you play, or make them just because crafting is so much fun!

TELESCOPE

Sailors used to navigate the seas using the stars in the night sky, so telescopes, or spyglasses, were an essential tool for any pirate.

found on page 17

YOU WILL NEED:
- THIN CARD • PAPER CUP • PLASTIC POCKET • STICKY TAPE • SCISSORS
- PAINT • PAINTBRUSH • GLUE STICK
- PENCIL

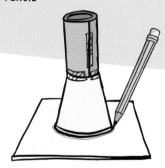

1. Roll up the thin card into a tube and stick in place. Make it the same size as the bottom of the paper cup.

2. Cut off the bottom of the cup and tape the tube to the hole.

3. Draw around the top of the cup, then draw a circle slightly bigger than it.

4. Cut the ring shape out. Stick some plastic on to the ring and stick this on to the end of the cup.

5. Paint the telescope and leave to dry before you use it.

TOP TIP
Draw a desert island scene on to the plastic so you can see it every time you look through the telescope.

SHIP'S RAT

A ship's rat is another name for the black rat, so-named because they were found on board many of the boats that sailed the seas. They moved fast and loved to climb, but most of the time they were looking for food that was stored in the wooden barrels.

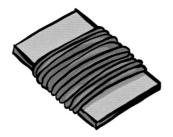

1. Wrap wool around a piece of square card.

2. Bend the card slightly so that it creates a gap and carefully remove the cardboard, keeping the wool as straight as possible.

4. Trim the pom-poms if necessary using scissors. Repeat so you have two pom-poms in total.

3. Wrap a long piece of wool around the middle and tie it tightly together to make a pom-pom.

5. Cut out ears, nose, feet and tail from felt or fabric scraps.

What shivers at the bottom of the ocean? A nervous wreck!

SQUEAK!

6. Stick the two pom-poms together and decorate with ears, nose, feet and a tail.

SHIPWRECK

The seas were once very dangerous places, with lots of cannons firing at enemy boats. If a boat sank, often its treasures sank with it. Lots of people still search for shipwrecks and their hidden treasures today, but you can make your very own.

1. Lie some lolly-pop sticks together so that they make a diamond.

2. Glue two more sticks on top, horizontally, so that the sticks all join together. You may need to trim them to size first.

3. Turn this over and build up the sides, gluing each layer in place until the sides are about 5 cm tall.

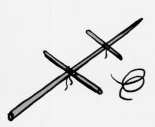

4. Use thread to make a cocktail stick mast.

5. Roll the modelling clay into a ball and use it to stick the mast in place.

CANNON

Cannons were popular weapons for boats, as they could be fired far and cause lots of damage. Gunpowder was lit at one end and the explosion would cause the cannon ball to be pushed out of the barrel with great force.

YOU WILL NEED:

- KITCHEN ROLL TUBE • BLACK PAINT
- BROWN PENS • PAINTBRUSH
- BLACK PAPER • TWO SPLIT PINS
- SCISSORS • THIN CARD

1. Cut up the tube so you have one longer piece and four small rings.

2. Paint all of these pieces black and leave to dry.

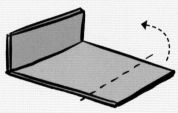

3. Make a square 'U' shape from the card and paint it to look like wood.

4. Use split pins to attach the tube to the 'U' shape. This lets you aim your cannon.

5. Stick the four rings to the sides to make the wheels. You can decorate these by sticking paper spokes to the outside of the rings.

PIRATE PARROT

Brightly-coloured macaws were valuable pets. Pirates often took them to sell in countries such as America. They were easy to transport as they were small and could be taught to repeat words or sounds out loud – making the long sea journeys much more fun!

YOU WILL NEED:
- ONE BRIGHTLY COLOURED SOCK
- WOOL • FABRIC GLUE • SCISSORS
- THICK CARD • SCRAP FABRIC

1. Half-fill one sock with scrap fabric and tie the open end with some wool.

2. Cut the tied end with scissors to make a feathery tail.

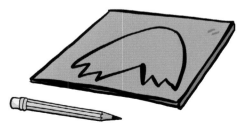

4. Cut out a triangle, two small circles and two wing shapes. Stick these to the sock using more fabric glue.

3. Make some feet from thick card and stick the stuffed sock to this using fabric glue. Leave to dry while you make the rest of the decorations.

PIECES OF EIGHT!

5. Make a headscarf and eyepatch from more scrap fabric and tie onto the sock parrot.

OCTOPUS WINDOW STICKER

Decorate your window to make a pirates' paradise. Start by making this simple octopus design and then choose what you would like to add next — make sunken treasures, shipwrecks or even shoals of tropical fish.

1. Draw your octopus design on to a piece of paper and then put it inside the plastic pocket.

YOU WILL NEED:
- WHITE CRAFT GLUE • GREEN FOOD COLOURING • WASHING-UP LIQUID
- PAINTBRUSH • PLASTIC POCKET
- BLACK PERMANENT MARKER PEN
- PAPER • PENCIL

2. Mix together 1 tablespoon of white craft glue with a drop of washing-up liquid and a drop of food colouring. Stir until the colour is even and not streaky.

3. Use the paintbrush to trace the design of the octopus directly on to the plastic. Make sure the layer of paint mixture is quite thick.

24 HOURS!

4. Leave to dry in a warm place for at least 24 hours before you draw the details on using the black marker pen.

5. Peel off the plastic and place on the window - it will stick all by itself!

PIRATE PUZZLE

CAN YOU FIND THE ANSWERS TO THESE QUESTIONS?

1. Which ship has discovered treasure?

2. How many fish are there?

3. Where is the parrot hiding?

4. Which ship has the most flags?

ANSWERS 1. Ship D **2.** 7 fish **3.** Ship B **4.** Ship C